LIFE *in the* OCEAN

The Story of Oceanographer
Sylvia Earle

CLAIRE A. NIVOLA

FRANCES FOSTER BOOKS

Farrar Straus Giroux

New York

For Po and his extraordinary Fish World,
and for Alycia and her inspired love of the natural world

With thanks to Dr. James McCarthy of Harvard University
for his careful attention and invaluable advice,
and to Sylvia Earle and her daughter, Liz,
for their support and encouragement throughout

Color separations by Bright Arts (HK) Ltd.
Printed in China by South China Printing Co. Ltd.,
Dongguan City, Guangdong Province
Designed by Roberta Pressel
First edition, 2012
5   7   9   10   8   6   4

mackids.com

Library of Congress Cataloging-in-Publication Data
Nivola, Claire A.
    Life in the ocean : the story of Sylvia Earle / Claire A. Nivola.
        p.   cm.
    Includes bibliographical references and index.
    ISBN: 978-0-374-38068-7 (alk. paper)
    1. Earle, Sylvia A., 1935–   —Juvenile literature.   2. Marine biologists—
United States—Juvenile literature.   3. Women marine biologists—United
States—Juvenile literature.   4. Women explorers—United States—Biography—
Juvenile literature.   I. Title.

QH91.3.E2N58 2012
551.46092—dc23
                                                                        2011016645

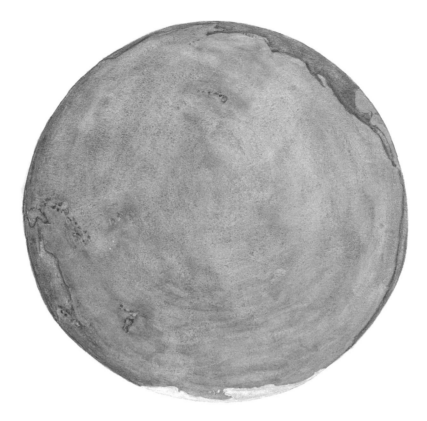

Seen from above, Earth's land seems to float like islands on a vast sea—there is so much more blue than green! Hidden below the surface of that ocean lies an immense watery world. Catching the sun's light at first, then cold and utterly black in its depths, the sea covers mountains taller, plains broader, and valleys steeper than any here on land.

Life came from the ocean long ago, and without the ocean none of us—neither you nor I—could survive a day. Living organisms in the sea release the oxygen we breathe in, and take up the carbon dioxide we breathe out. Along with the plants on land, the ocean forms the lungs of our planet, breathing in and out. Its surface evaporates to form the marvelous clouds that give us rain and snow. Its temperature shapes the weather patterns we live by. And it is home to more life-forms and surprising creatures—from its shallows to its deepest depths—than we have here on land. Sylvia Earle, who has spent more than seven thousand hours underwater, calls the ocean "the blue heart of the planet."

Sylvia began her early childhood inland, on an old farm just outside
Paulsboro, New Jersey. Her mother and father bought the place when
Sylvia was three years old so that she and her two brothers could grow
up in the country just as their parents had done.

Even when she was very small, Sylvia spent hours outdoors exploring
on her own. She was far too curious to be afraid. There were so many

living creatures in every inch of the nearby woods—in the farm's pond, in its creek, and among the gnarled trees and grapevines of its orchard— that she never felt alone. Sylvia's parents planted apple, pear, and walnut trees and a large vegetable garden. Countless butterflies visited the flowers of the garden, and the fragrance of the lilac bushes in May made one's head spin.

Little Sylvia would sit by herself—
very still and for a very long time—waiting
and watching to see what was going on
in the pond, or under a fallen tree in the
woods. Her mother called these outings
"investigations." In a notebook, Sylvia
described what she saw. The windowsills of
the house were lined with her collection
jars, which held tadpoles, salamanders,
insects, and plants. Sylvia said she was a
biologist and a botanist long before she even
knew what those words meant.

When Sylvia was twelve, her family moved to Florida. Gone would
be the pond teeming with life in summer and glazed with ice for skating
in winter. Gone her beloved pony and quarter horse, the orchard, creek,
and woods. How hard it was to leave! And yet Sylvia could not possibly
have imagined what awaited her as they drove up the dead-end street to

their new home north of Clearwater. There before her lay the vast, broad
sea. In New Jersey she had visited the Atlantic Ocean, but this water was
a clear blue-green, and it was warm and calm—the Gulf of Mexico right
in her own backyard! It was then, her mother said, that Sylvia "lost her
heart to the water."

That birthday, Sylvia was given a pair of swim goggles. Floating on the surface of the grassy water, she began her "investigations" all over again—finding tiny crabs, darting fish, and the occasional sea horse that reminded her of the horse and pony she had left behind. Meeting all these new creatures, she said, "softened the blow of leaving the farm." How could she feel lonely when every "spoonful" of water was filled with life!

In the library she found books by the naturalist William Beebe describing his descent into the deep ocean in his "bathysphere" some thirty years earlier. Sylvia wanted to see what he had seen with her *own* eyes, and, as she grew up, it seemed that nothing was going to stop her.

When Sylvia was only five she had climbed unafraid into a single passenger seat behind the pilot of a small plane and flown up and over the field where her parents watched, amazed.

From the age of sixteen, when she swam thirty feet to the bottom of a river using diving gear for the first time—

to scuba diving while researching algae for her university degree,

to joining an expedition where she was the only woman among seventy men on a research ship in the Indian Ocean,

to leading a team of divers stationed for
two weeks in a deep-sea laboratory off
the U.S. Virgin Islands,

to walking on the ocean floor
in an aqua suit that looked like
a space suit,

to descending 3,000 feet in the
Pacific Ocean in a one-person
spherical bubble she had helped
to design,

to plunging 13,000 feet underwater in
a Japanese submersible—Sylvia never
stopped trying to dive deeper and see more.

Again and again she has emerged from her dives to tell us what she has seen.

She describes creatures who do not fear her, but rather look at her with the same curiosity she has for them. Take the humpback whale, forty feet long and weighing 80,000 pounds, who, on the first day of a three-month whale study, swam straight at her, like a freight train bearing down on a mouse. Moments before the collision, the whale swerved gracefully, tilting her great head to look into Sylvia's eyes with her own "grapefruit-size" eyes as she slid past inches away at high speed. By the second day the whales were waiting for the boat; as Sylvia dove into the water, their dark shapes instantly swam swiftly toward her from below. "From the start," Sylvia said, "I found myself being observed by them."

Pictures of whales, says Sylvia, make them look "big and fat and ponderous and lumpy . . . Whales are like swallows . . . like otters . . . They move in any direction. They swim upside down. They're vertical. They're every which way . . . They are sleek and elegant and gorgeous, among the most exquisite creatures on the planet. They move like ballerinas . . . Rollicking, frolicking creatures, doing all this wonderful dancing in the sea."

Sylvia has even heard whales singing while she has been underwater, and, once, the force of the sound waves made her entire body vibrate and shake. Wavelengths of light do not penetrate deep into water, but sound waves travel four times faster in water than in air, so whales can communicate across vast distances. Sylvia says that hearing their haunting and beautiful songs in the sea is like being inside the heart of an orchestra.

So much of diving is an all-too-brief glimpse below the surface. Sylvia had always wanted to know what it was like to *live* in the sea, to be a part of the daily life of the underwater world. She finally had a chance to do just that when she spent two weeks fifty feet below at the deep-sea station Tektite II. For as many as twelve hours a day, she swam among the fish and coral reefs, watching the changeover from day to night and back again. Using a small flashlight at night, she noticed that the day fish "tucked in" to the same nooks and crevices the night fish had just vacated, each fish often returning time and again to its same resting place—just as we do!

Among others, Sylvia came to know the five gray angelfish she saw each day: one shy, one more aggressive, some, like her, full of curiosity. She observed the whole cast of characters—squirrelfish, triggerfish, parrot fish—that came and went in the course of a day and night, the way you get to know a neighborhood if you keep your ears and eyes and heart open. Just as no two people are alike, no two creatures of the sea

are alike. And yet we all have so much in common! Think of eating and digestion, Sylvia reminds us: "Lobsters do it, horseshoe crabs do it, sharks do it, we do it."

Of that time, she has said, "I'm changed forever because I lived underwater for two weeks in 1970. I wish that everybody could go live underwater if only for a day."

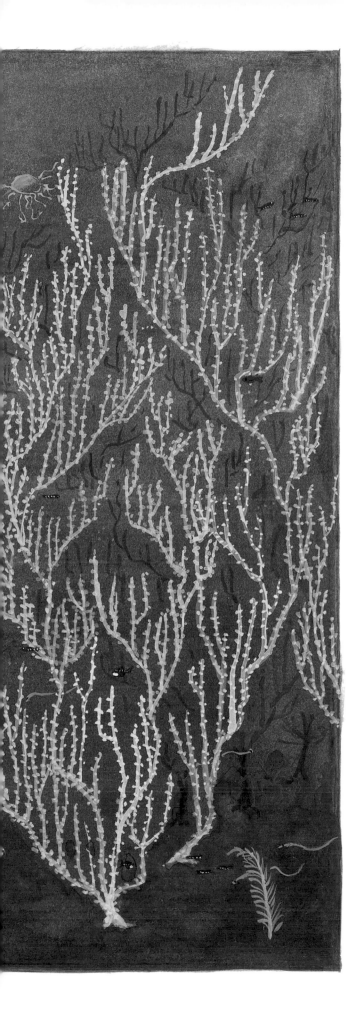

Sylvia was just as eager to travel as far down as possible into the deepest ocean. The walk she took in the Jim suit nine years after her stay among the coral reefs was on the ocean floor off Hawaii, 1,250 feet down—deeper than anyone has ever walked! She had imagined, as we might, too, that it would be black darkness down there. If she had gone another 1,600 feet down it would have been, but here, to her delight, the midday sun still sifted its blue light-waves through the clear ocean water and she found herself in a magical twilight of deep indigo. "There weren't stars visible . . . but there were bioluminescent creatures flashing with their blue fire."

From the ocean floor sprang a field of bamboo coral, some stalks taller than she was. When she touched the top of the long, pale spirals, "little blue donuts of light" pulsed down them; when she touched them at the bottom, the same pulses moved upward, ring after ring of light.

Every spoonful of water in the deep ocean,
Sylvia says, is brimming with extraordinary
forms of life. Creatures, each in their own
way, sparkle and flash with lights of their
own, like fireflies here on land!

One expedition, 3,000 feet down, was, Sylvia says,

like "diving into a galaxy."

We have explored only 5 percent of the ocean. We know more about the planets in outer space than we know about the sea on our very own home planet! Sylvia Earle believes that if we do not learn about the ocean world we will never really *care about* it or *take care of* it.

When you next look out over the ocean, stop to think of the vast mountains, valleys, and plains below its surface. Think of how it breathes and gives us life. And think of all the wondrous creatures it holds in its waters—from whales, to busy, colorful coral reefs, to those living firework displays that light up the cold, black waters of its mysterious depths.

Hawksbill Sea Turtle

Caribbean Reef Squid

Lined Sea Horse

Portuguese Man-of-War Jellyfish

Pacific Blue Tang

French Butterflyfish

Golden Damselfish

Spotted Soapfish

Harlequin Tusk Fish

Blue Parrot Fish

Butter Hamlet

AUTHOR'S NOTE

As soon as Sylvia Earle began her "investigations" in the clear waters of the Gulf of Mexico, she dreamed of "going deeper, staying longer." The challenge of finding ways to provide the oxygen needed to breathe while under the tremendous pressure of the sea later led Sylvia to start three companies and a nonprofit foundation aimed at designing and building systems that can explore the deep ocean. Becoming an entrepreneur, and facing obstacles along the way, in part because she is a woman, are a large part of her story. For some, Sylvia Earle's life serves as an inspiring example of a woman who, in pursuing her passion, has defied conventional expectations at every stage of her life. In fact, her life should be viewed as a remarkable list of achievements for *any* marine scientist: setting diving depth records, serving as chief scientist of the National Oceanic and Atmospheric Administration (NOAA), serving as Explorer in Residence at the National Geographic Society, consulting as a world expert on oil spills, and writing and speaking widely on the plight of the ocean.

But Sylvia Earle's accomplishments have always been in the service of her lifelong passion: to witness firsthand the marvels of the sea and, increasingly, to serve as a spokeswoman for the vital importance of the ocean to the health of our planet and to our very survival.

Sylvia Earle would like us all to delight as much as she does in the underwater world, in the ingenuity and variety of our fellow creatures who dwell there. But she has also seen close-up how the ocean is suffering at our hands. She believes it is our ignorance of what is at stake that is in large part to blame.

Sylvia was born in 1935. Most of the damage done to the ocean has taken place during her lifetime. In less than a century, a sea world that has been in the making for some three and a half billion years is being altered by human activity.

Explosive human population growth combined with modern fishing technologies has emptied the ocean of 90 percent of its big fish and depleted its numbers of turtles, sharks, tuna, and whales. More than eighty million metric tons of ocean wildlife are fished each year, and for every fish caught and sent to market, quantities of other, "less valued" fish are killed and discarded as waste. Not only are we using up our marine food source, we are diminishing the biodiversity that all life depends on.

Our use of oil for energy has made it a routine matter that thousands of oil spills take place in the ocean each year. The famous *Exxon Valdez* spill in the

Reticulated Moray Eel

Banded Pipefish

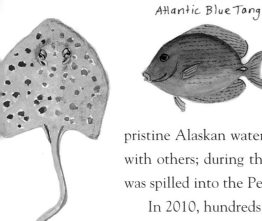

Blue-spotted
Stingray

Atlantic Blue Tang

Spotfin Butterflyfish

Striped Bass

Blue-ringed Angelfish

Six-line Soapfish

Squirrelfish

Ocean Surgeonfish

Spotted Trunkfish

Blue Chromis
Damselfish

pristine Alaskan waters of Prince William Sound in 1989 was minor compared with others; during the Gulf War, two years later, forty-five times as much oil was spilled into the Persian Gulf.

In 2010, hundreds of millions of gallons of crude oil poured into the Gulf of Mexico, the ocean waters Sylvia had snorkeled in so happily as a child. During that disaster, an unprecedented two million gallons of toxic dispersants were used to break down the oil. As Sylvia testified before Congress, these chemicals make "the ocean look a little better on the surface—where most people are—but make circumstances a lot worse under the surface . . . [where sea creatures] are awash in a lethal brew of oil and butoxyethanol."

Into our ocean, all around the world, we have dumped lethal nuclear waste, industrial waste, pollutants from underwater mining, and just plain garbage. We abandon sunken ships and allow our highways, farms, fields, and yards to leach fertilizers, pesticides, and other chemicals into freshwater systems leading to coastal waters and on to the sea at large. Are we thinking that the sea is vast and deep enough to take all this and more? Plastic breaks down into smaller pieces but does not disappear altogether; there are areas of the ocean that contain more plastic than living plankton. The ocean is simply *not* big enough.

And we have filled the sea with new sounds, too—drilling, explosions, boat engines, sonar. For creatures like the whales in this story, exquisitely sensitive to sound waves, these human interferences can cause great suffering, disorientation, strandings, possibly even death.

Since the Industrial Revolution in the early nineteenth century, the ocean has generously taken up 50 percent of the carbon we have released into the atmosphere. But as we burn more and more fossil fuels, the carbon in the ocean increases, and so, too, does acidification, a change in the ocean chemistry that makes it more difficult for corals, mollusks, and other sea creatures to form the skeletons that protect them. Moreover, as the climate warms, there is concern that the release of methane, a potent, heat-trapping gas stored deep in the frozen sea-floor sediments, could further accelerate the warming of our planet.

Sylvia Earle has written, "Looking into the eyes of a wild dolphin—who is looking into mine—inspires me to learn everything I can about them and do everything I can to take care of them . . . You can't care if you don't know."

Garden Eels

Royal Gramma

Cleaner Goby

Bluefin Tuna

Banded Butterflyfish

SELECTED BIBLIOGRAPHY

Baker, Beth. *Sylvia Earle: Guardian of the Sea*. Minneapolis: Lerner Publications, 2001.

Earle, Sylvia A. *Dive: My Adventures in the Deep Frontier*. Washington, D.C.: National Geographic Society, 1991.

————. *Sea Change: A Message of the Oceans*. New York: G.P. Putnam's Sons, 1995.

————. *Sea Critters*. Washington, D.C.: National Geographic Society, 2000.

————. "Sylvia Earle's Life Aquatic." Interview by Tom Ashbrook. *On Point with Tom Ashbrook*, WBUR and NPR, February 9, 2009.

————. "Sylvia Earle: Undersea Explorer." Interview, January 27, 1991, www.achievement.org/autodoc/printmember/ear0int-1.

————. *The World Is Blue: How Our Fate and the Ocean's Are One*. Washington, D.C.: National Geographic Society, 2009.

Earle, Sylvia A., and Linda K. Glover. *Ocean: An Illustrated Atlas*. Washington, D.C.: National Geographic Society, 2009.

Nouvian, Claire. *The Deep: The Extraordinary Creatures of the Abyss*. Chicago: University of Chicago Press, 2009.

Siebert, Charles. "What Are Whales Trying to Tell Us?" *The New York Times Magazine*, July 12, 2009, 28–45.